BREATHE OUT
ATHE OUT BREAT
REATHE OUT BR
HE OUT BREATHE IN BREAT
BREATHE OUT BREATHE IN
ATHE OUT BREATHE IN BRE
BREATHE OUT BREATHE IN
THE OUT BREATHE IN BREAT
BREATHE OUT BREATHE IN
THE OUT BREATHE IN BREA
REATHE OUT BREATHE IN
HE OUT BREATHE IN BREAT
BREATHE OUT BREATHE IN
ATHE OUT BREATHE IN BRE
BREATHE OUT BREATHE IN
THE OUT BREATHE IN BREA
BREATHE OUT BREATHE IN
ATHE OUT BREATHE IN BREA
REATHE OUT BREATHE IN
HE OUT BREATHE IN BREAT
BREATHE OUT BREATHE IN

BREATHE THROUGH IT

An Interactive Guide to Ease Your Anxiety Through
Meditation, Visualization, and Breathwork

By
Carissa Potter
and Vera Kachouh

Tarcher
an imprint of Penguin Random House
New York

Tarcher

an imprint of Penguin Random House LLC
1745 Broadway, New York, NY 10019
penguinrandomhouse.com

Most Tarcher books are available at a discount when purchased in quantity for sales promotions or
corporate use. Special editions, which include personalized covers, excerpts, and corporate imprints,
can be created when purchased in large quantities. For more information, please e-mail specialmarkets
@penguinrandomhouse.com. Your local bookstore can also assist with discounted bulk purchases using
the Penguin Random House corporate Business-to-Business program. For assistance in locating a
participating retailer, e-mail B2B@penguinrandomhouse.com.

Library of Congress Cataloging-in-Publication Data

Names: Potter, Carissa, author. | Kachouh, Vera, author.
Title: Breathe through it : an interactive guide to ease your anxiety through meditation, visualization,
and breathwork / [Carissa Potter, Vera Kachouh].
Description: [New York] : Tarcher, [2025]
Identifiers: LCCN 2024044562 | ISBN 9780593719053 (trade paperback)
Subjects: LCSH: Meditation. | Anxiety.
Classification: LCC BF637.M4 P68 2025 | DDC 158.1/2—dc23/eng/20250208
LC record available at https://lccn.loc.gov/2024044562

Printed in the United States of America
1st Printing

The authorized representative in the EU for product safety and compliance is Penguin Random House Ireland,
Morrison Chambers, 32 Nassau Street, Dublin D02 YH68, Ireland, https://eu-contact.penguin.ie.

THIS PRACTICE BELONGS TO:

Here you are, breathing.

I CAN DO
HARD THINGS.
I TRUST IN THE
RANDOMNESS
OF LIFE. THAT
SOME THINGS
ARE OUT OF
MY CONTROL.

I TAKE COMFORT IN THE PAST. I HAVE MANY DATA POINTS THAT SUGGEST I WILL MAKE IT THROUGH.

INTRODUCTION

what is breath?

We need breath to live.

It is a part of every moment of every day, in our waking world and in our dreams. In every interaction, thought, stroke of the keyboard, kiss for a loved one, song sung, and heartbreak felt, there it is—the breath.

Breath is our constant, quiet companion. It can seem like nothing more than a background to existence, a static that is easy enough to tune out and ignore. If we are living, we are breathing. But what if we tuned in to our breath and began to notice it? What if we could turn up the volume on the breath, offer it our thanks, even?

When we think about it carefully, everything is breath, but somehow, it also can be viewed separately from us or at a distance. It can be isolated and thought about. It can become the subject of a book, like this one. It can be practiced. Breath is the thread that weaves together all other possibilities. We notice breath when it is stripped from us. We notice it when it falls short. Swimming underwater, we hold our breath to the point of danger; we feel its lack pressing into us. We gasp for air. We surface and gulp it greedily. Our lungs push against that boundary. Something inside us says, it's time—*breathe*.

During the early days of the COVID-19 pandemic, we kept our breath away from one another as an act of care. We watched in horror as George Floyd was murdered by police, asking for breath, asking for his mother. This invisible force, breath, is robbed from us during wildfire season, when breathing the air—made visible by smoke—can be deadly.

Some people suffer from chronic diseases of the lungs and find themselves gasping for air as an aspect of daily existence.

Breath can be taken, and breath can be given. When we are scared, excited, turned on, or anxious, our breath changes. It shallows or quickens or heaves or halts. Breath rises and falls in our chests whether we notice it or not. On any given day, our breath transforms. Begin to notice your breath, and it reads like a barometer of mood. *I can't breathe* as a metaphor for *I feel trapped*. *I'm suffocating* as a metaphor for *I need to change my life*.

Breath is a country, and all living beings are its citizens. Breath is there for us when nothing else is. It is something that all the living share, that each of us can access when we are in pain.

We take about 12 breaths per minute. Within each of those breaths lies a possibility: to feel better. To notice, to slow down or speed up, to sink deeper into yourself.

This book is a guide to breathing. Because breathing is living, this book also is a guide to living. It is a way of noticing your life and filling your lungs with the air of it; to expand your idea of what life is and what it can be; to elongate the moment, and in doing so, to lengthen the sense of the time that we have here on Earth, alive and breathing.

In every 60 seconds, we have roughly 12 opportunities to shape how we will meet the moment and who we will be when we get there, just by breathing through it.

TIME & TIMED EXERCISES

This book is organized into sections based on the amount of time you may want to spend on a breathing exercise—1 minute, 5 minutes, 10 minutes, or 60 minutes. Use the time you have, and flip between the sections however you like.

Notice how the exercises alter your experience of time itself. Some short exercises might feel long, and some long ones might feel short if you enter a flow state. The fact that each section has a time frame is also a reminder that you don't need a lot of time to make these exercises work for you. Remember, you are breathing all the time. Even 1 minute a day—or just 1 deep breath a day—can make a difference.

Over time, you might notice that you don't need or want to be conscious of the time during a breathing exercise. With practice, you may find yourself just dropping into an exercise on the fly and finishing only when it feels right to stop.

BENEFITS OF BREATHING EXERCISES

The exercises collected in this book are inspired by a vast range of influences, from yoga and Pranayama (breathwork) to contemporary art (see Marina Abramović) to Lamaze for giving birth. They are merged with our own life (and breath) experiences. Take this blend of influences as an invitation to put your own stamp on the exercises. They inevitably will become yours anyway, as you breathe through your body in the singular time and space that it occupies.

All the exercises are about feeling better, but that is, at best, a slippery concept. For us, two women living in the twenty-first century, the single most important thing that breathing intentionally does is get us out of our heads.

Humans simply weren't meant to consume the amount of information and sensory inputs that we confront on a daily basis. Breathing moves us past the doom spiral of our thoughts, the news, and the endless to-do lists, and situates us back into the realm of our bodies, where things unfold more slowly, at a terrestrial pace.

Scientific research shows that breathing exercises have tangible, positive effects on our health, like these:

Reduced stress and anxiety
Lower blood pressure
Improved focus
Increased creativity
Regulated moods and fewer mood swings
Increased oxygen intake leading to better brain function
Decreased fight-or-flight response due to reduced cortisol
Better sleep

BEFORE YOU BEGIN

"Wellness" culture wants you to believe that your problems can be solved with the right yoga pose or breathing technique. Life is much more complicated than that, and we exist within structures that directly inhibit our wellness. If your basic needs aren't met, no amount of deep breathing will solve things. Abraham Maslow created a hierarchy of needs that illuminates this, shown opposite.

If we don't have food, shelter, water, and sleep, we can't access creativity, confidence, morality, and spirituality.

Before you begin these exercises, take a beat to consider the basics: Have I slept, eaten, and showered? Am I in a safe environment? Am I thirsty? Do I need to poop? Go ahead and tend to your most basic functions first.

WHY DOES EVERYTHING FEEL SO OFF?

self-actualization (the process of becoming what you are capable of...)

respect, selfesteem, status, freedom

friendship, family, intimacy, connection

employment, health, property, security, etc.

air, water, food, shelter, sleep, clothing, reproduction

IN THIS MOMENT, WE ARE ALL DESTABILIZED...

WELL-BEING CHECK

What are some external factors that might be interfering with your wellness right now? Are you under financial stress? Is the weather dreary? Do you have a need that is not being met? Acknowledge what these factors are, and write them down here.

Today I am feeling:

The weather outside is:

Season:

moon phase:

stress level:

1 2 3 4 5 6 7 8 9 10

☐ I'm hydrated
☐ I got enough sleep
☐ I've eaten
☐ I've moved my body
☐ I've connected
☐ I've pooped
☐ I've spent time outside

Write down what you are feeling grateful for:

Now, get yourself into a comfortable position. Put a hand to your chest, and whisper to yourself, "I love you."

Flip to any page and begin.

GUIDE TO VISUAL CUES

These visual cues are a quick way to orient yourself in an exercise to know if it's something you can carry out in the moment you find yourself in. If you need to have your eyes closed, for example, or be lying down in a dark room, save those exercises for when they make sense situationally.

All the exercises in this book are given a time frame— 1 minute, 5 minutes, 10 minutes, or 60 minutes. Flip the book on its spine to clearly see which exercises will take more time than others. (Look for the black band.)

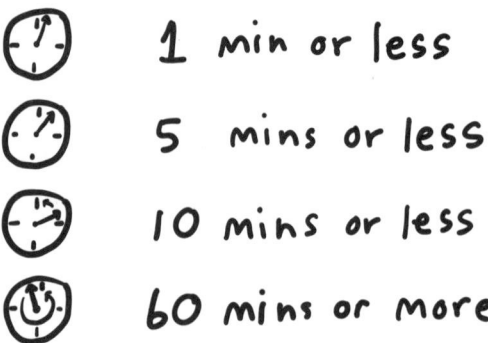

1 min or less

5 mins or less

10 mins or less

60 mins or more

sitting   eyes closed

standing   eyes open

on all fours   outdoors

day   indoors

night   reflections

lying down

WHATEVER IT IS
THAT KEEPS ME
GOING THROUGH
THE HARD STUFF
HAS LEFT MY
BODY...

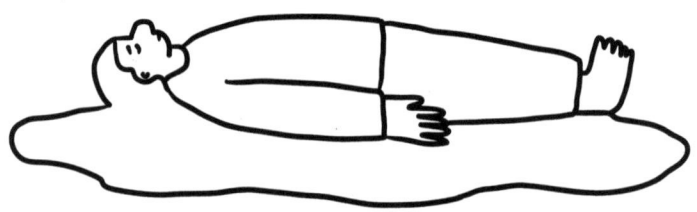

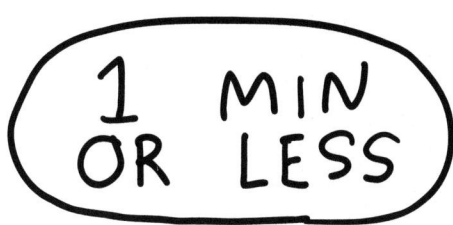

BEE BREATH

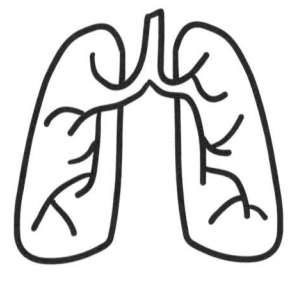

Inhale through your nose.

Keep going until your lungs feel full.

Breathe out with a
buzzing sound, like
a bee, for as long
as you can.

Repeat.

Variation:
Put your thumbs over your ears
and your fingers over your eyes.
Hum instead of buzzing on the exhale.

fold here so you can return →

NOTES

BEFORE I FELT:

AFTER I FEEL:

NEXT TIME I'D CHANGE:

UP-DOWN BREATH

Close your eyes.

Inhale deeply through your nose.

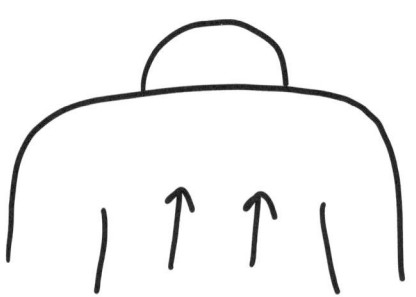

Lift your shoulders up to your ears as you inhale.

Exhale through your mouth with a loud HAH sound.

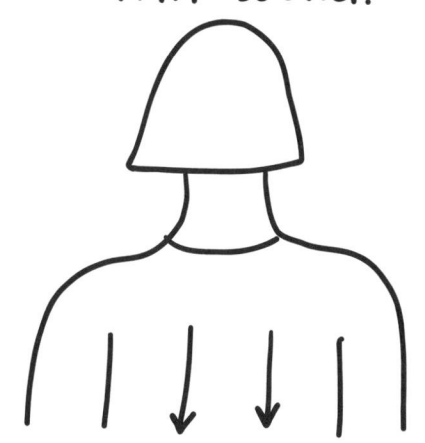

Drop your shoulders down as you exhale. Repeat.

fold here so you can return →

NOTES

BEFORE I FELT:

AFTER I FEEL:

NEXT TIME I'D CHANGE:

BOAT SEND-OFF

Picture
what's upsetting
or worrying you.

Once the image feels
clear, put it into a boat.

Say goodbye to the worry and send it off.

Watch it depart, moving away from your body...

until it disappears completely from view.

fold here so you can return →

NOTES

BEFORE I FELT:

AFTER I FEEL:

NEXT TIME I'D CHANGE:

CAT / COW

Begin in a tabletop position. Stack your wrists under your shoulders and your knees under your hips.

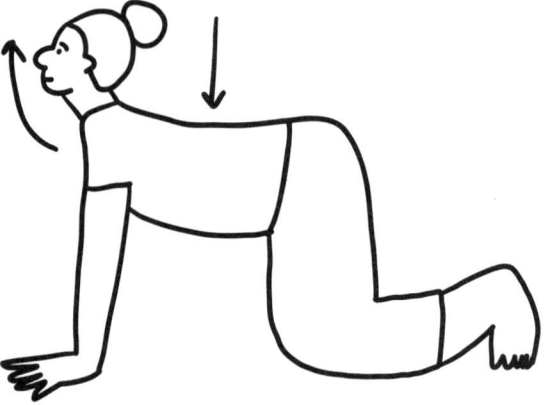

Take a deep inhale while dropping your belly toward the floor and tilting your head up toward the ceiling, like a cow.

Exhale fully while slowly bringing your belly up into a curve, like a cat, and tucking your head down, looking toward your belly button.

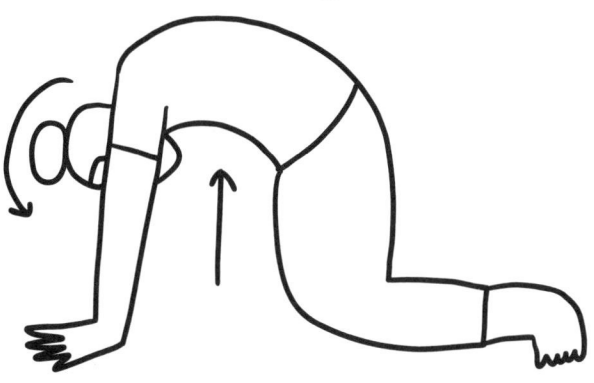

Repeat several times.
move slowly.
Use your breath to guide each motion.

fold here so you can return →

NOTES

BEFORE I FELT:

AFTER I FEEL:

NEXT TIME I'D CHANGE:

LION'S BREATH

Find a
comfortable
seat.

Inhale through
your nose.

Open your mouth to exhale. As you exhale,

Stick your tongue out and make a "roar" sound.

Repeat 3 times.

Variation:
Take a natural breath in between each Lion's Breath and continue for up to 3 minutes, alternating between one roar and one natural exhale.

fold here so you can return →

NOTES

BEFORE I FELT:

AFTER I FEEL:

NEXT TIME I'D CHANGE:

SMELL THE FLOWERS, BLOW OUT THE CANDLES

Close your eyes.

Imagine a flower
in full bloom

Take a deep breath in
through your nose and
smell the flower.

Round your lips as you
exhale slowly through
your mouth, as if
blowing out a candle.

Variation:
Add a wish as you blow out the candle.
Visualize your hope as clearly as you can.

fold here so you can return →

NOTES

BEFORE I FELT:

AFTER I FEEL:

NEXT TIME I'D CHANGE:

BOX BREATHING

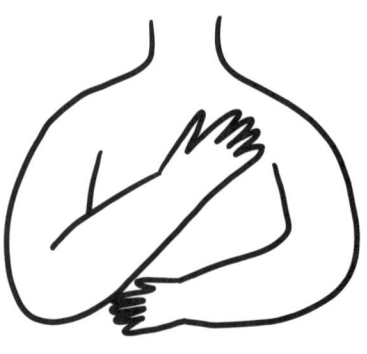

Place your
right hand
on your heart

and

your left hand
on your belly.

1. Inhale deeply for 4 seconds.

2. Hold your breath for 4 seconds.

3. Exhale your breath for 4 seconds.

4. Wait 4 seconds before your next inhale.

Repeat 4 times.

fold here so you can return →

NOTES

BEFORE I FELT:

AFTER I FEEL:

NEXT TIME I'D CHANGE:

BUTTERFLY HUG

Close your eyes and
cross both arms
over your chest.

Breathe in and
out slowly.

Find your collarbones and begin tapping, alternating fingers as if playing a piano very quickly.

tap tap

Continue tapping while breathing slowly and deeply until you feel your energy shift.

fold here so you can return →

NOTES

BEFORE I FELT:

AFTER I FEEL:

NEXT TIME I'D CHANGE:

<u>A</u> <u>SIP</u> <u>OF</u> <u>WATER</u>

Fill a glass with water and find a comfortable seat.

Take a deep breath. Slowly sip the water.

As it moves down your throat, imagine it pulling the stress with it, carrying it away.

Let the cool feeling of the water wash away what's troubling you.

Repeat with each sip.

fold here so you can return →

NOTES

BEFORE I FELT:

AFTER I FEEL:

NEXT TIME I'D CHANGE:

IT IS NOT YOUR FAULT.

<u>3</u> <u>INEXPLICABLY</u> <u>BEAUTIFUL</u> <u>THINGS</u>

Close your eyes. Take a long, deep breath.

Open your eyes and look around without expectation until something beautiful catches your eye.

Let your attention rest on
the beautiful object.

marvel in the colors,
shapes, story, etc.

What's beautiful about it?

Repeat twice more,
finding 2 more things
to look at deeply.

fold here so you can return →

NOTES

BEFORE I FELT:

AFTER I FEEL:

NEXT TIME I'D CHANGE:

CHILD'S POSE

Kneel on the floor. Tuck your calves under your thighs, and touch your big toes together.

Take a deep inhale. As you exhale, fold your torso over your thighs.

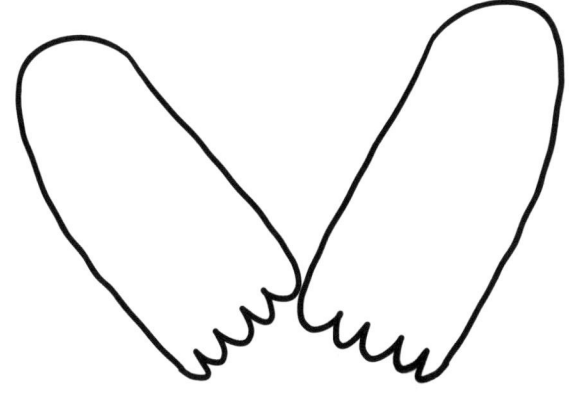

Place your arms out in front of you, or rest them to either side, with your forehead kissing the floor.

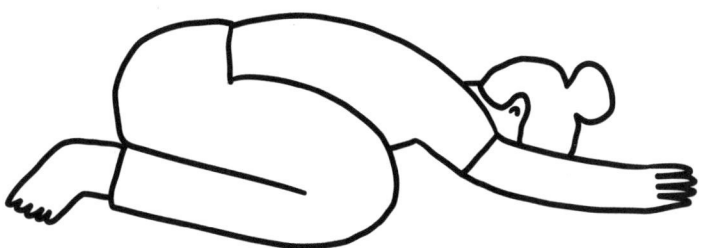

Breathe naturally.

fold here so you can return →

NOTES

BEFORE I FELT:

AFTER I FEEL:

NEXT TIME I'D CHANGE:

GROUNDING PRACTICE

Sit or stand. Make sure your feet are in contact with the ground. Take off your shoes if you can.

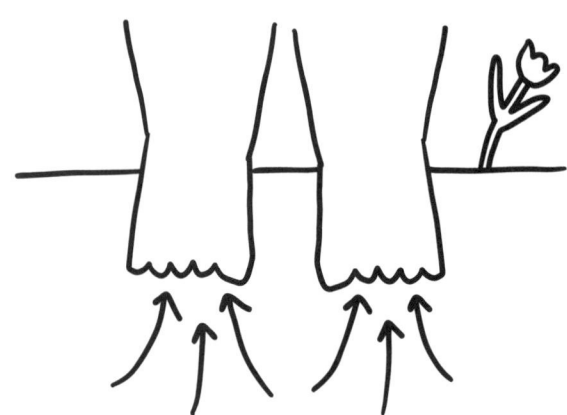

Close your eyes. Feel your feet pressing into the ground, making sure every toe has contact. Envision the ground coming up to meet the soles of your feet.

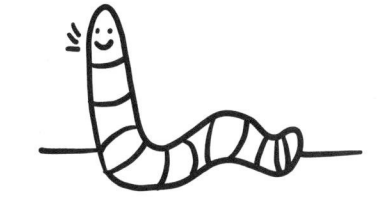

Repeat to yourself:

MY FEET ARE ON THE GROUND.

Continue to focus on your feet on the solid ground, repeating the mantra, until the feeling of acute stress fades.

fold here so you can return →

NOTES

BEFORE I FELT:

AFTER I FEEL:

NEXT TIME I'D CHANGE:

BELLY BREATH

Lie on your back.

Place one hand on your chest and the other hand on your belly.

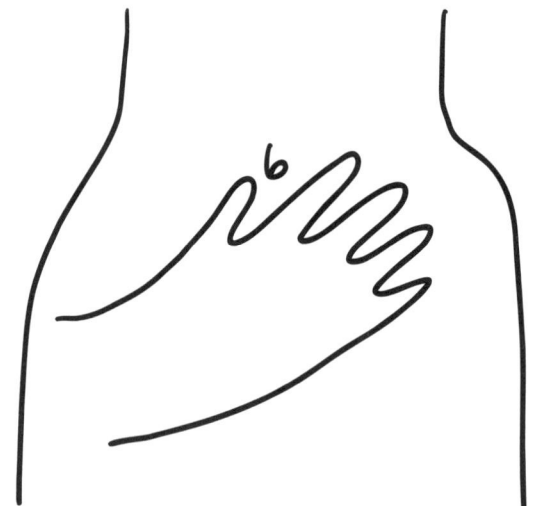

Inhale deeply through your nose, filling your belly with as much air as you can.

Try to keep your chest still, as you feel your stomach expand like a balloon.

Hold your breath for a moment at the top of the inhale.

Exhale slowly through your mouth, feeling your belly deflate.

Repeat.

fold here so you can return →

NOTES

BEFORE I FELT:

AFTER I FEEL:

NEXT TIME I'D CHANGE:

FOLDING INWARD

Sit down on the floor.
You can cushion yourself
with a blanket if you like.

Wrap your arms around
your legs, grasping your
opposite forearm in
each hand.

Tilt your head, resting your forehead on your knees.

Breathe deeply. Notice the warmth your own body creates.

Notice how you are held.

fold here so you can return →

NOTES

BEFORE I FELT:

AFTER I FEEL:

NEXT TIME I'D CHANGE:

MUSCLE RELAXATION

Find a comfortable seat.

Rest your hands on your lap.

Close your eyes.
Take a deep breath in.

Make a tight fist with
each hand.

Squeeze your nails
into your palms.

Notice the tension in your
fists as you hold this
for a few breaths.

Open your hands. Let go of
all that tension.

fold here so you can return →

NOTES

BEFORE I FELT:

AFTER I FEEL:

NEXT TIME I'D CHANGE:

SINGING PRACTICE TO GET INTO YOUR BODY

Pick a song you love to belt out.

Press play.

Inhale deeply through your nose.

Sing along
as loudly
as you can.

Fill your lungs
with song.

fold here so you can return →

NOTES

BEFORE I FELT:

AFTER I FEEL:

NEXT TIME I'D CHANGE:

<u>3-3-3</u>
<u>FOR</u> <u>ANXIETY</u>

Sit down.
Close your eyes and
take a deep breath.

Open your eyes and
identify 3 objects.

Now listen for 3 sounds.

Now move 3 parts of your body.

End with a deep inhale and full exhale.

fold here so you can return →

NOTES

BEFORE I FELT:

AFTER I FEEL:

NEXT TIME I'D CHANGE:

COLD PLUNGE

Prepare an ice bath large enough for your face.

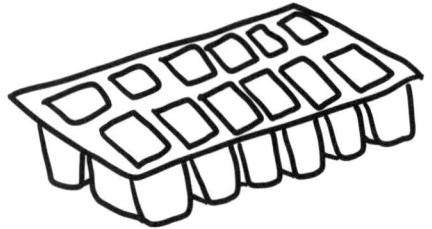

Make sure the water is really cold by adding ice cubes.

Plunge your face into the water for 5-to 10-second intervals.

Take breaks when
you need to,
breathing deeply
between plunges.

fold here so you can return →

NOTES

BEFORE I FELT:

AFTER I FEEL:

NEXT TIME I'D CHANGE:

PERMISSION TO SAVOR
ANY MOMENTS OF
JOY YOU CAN FIND...

BODY SCAN

Lie down.
Close your eyes.

Starting from your toes, bring awareness to each part of your body.

Move up your body very slowly, imagining that as you encounter each part, it softens and turns to jelly.

Toes, feet, ankles,
calves, knees, thighs,
butt, hips, tummy,
chest, arms, armpits,
neck, all parts of
the face and head.

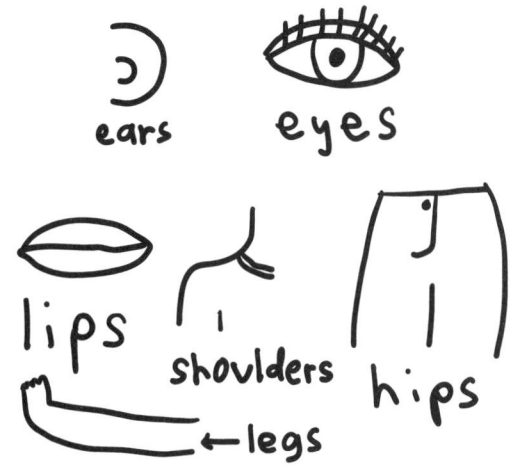

ears   eyes

lips   shoulders   hips
        ←legs

Rest where you are until it
feels right to move.

fold here so you can return →

Focus your attention on your body. Use this to record any tender spots.

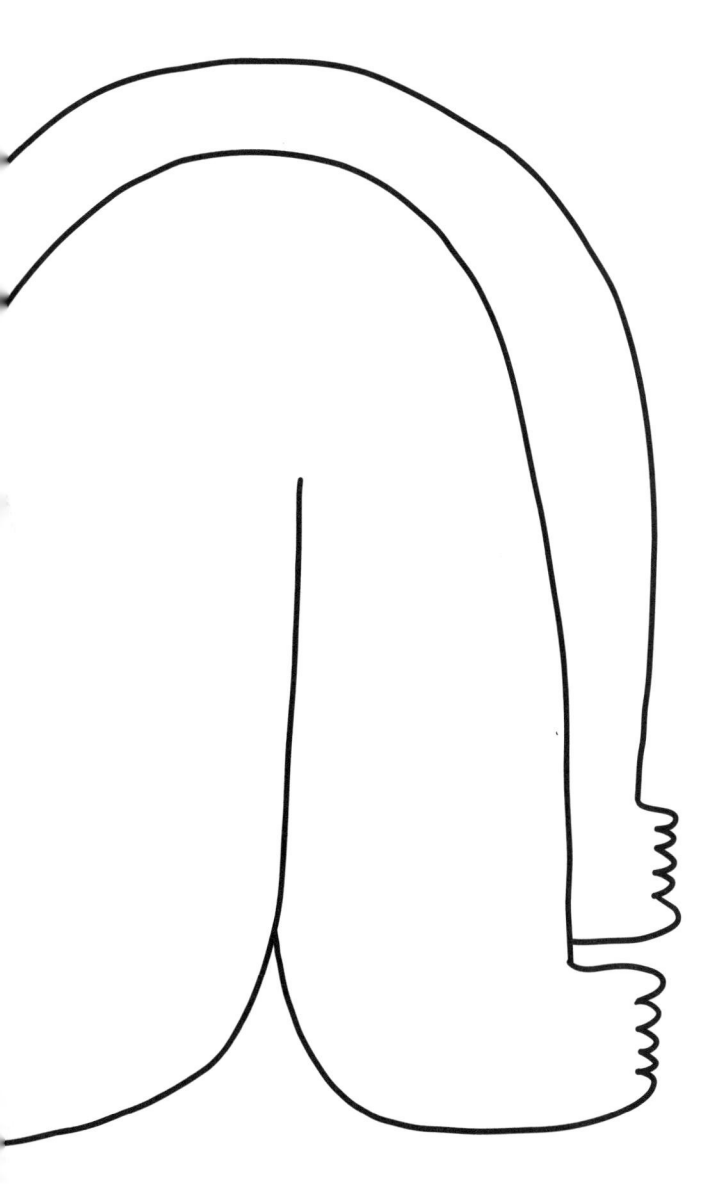

NOTES

BEFORE I FELT:

AFTER I FEEL:

NEXT TIME I'D CHANGE:

START COLORING

Take a deep breath.
Tell yourself: The only
thing I have to do
right now is color
this page.

Begin, using whatever
materials you have on
hand.

Choose colors that
soothe you.

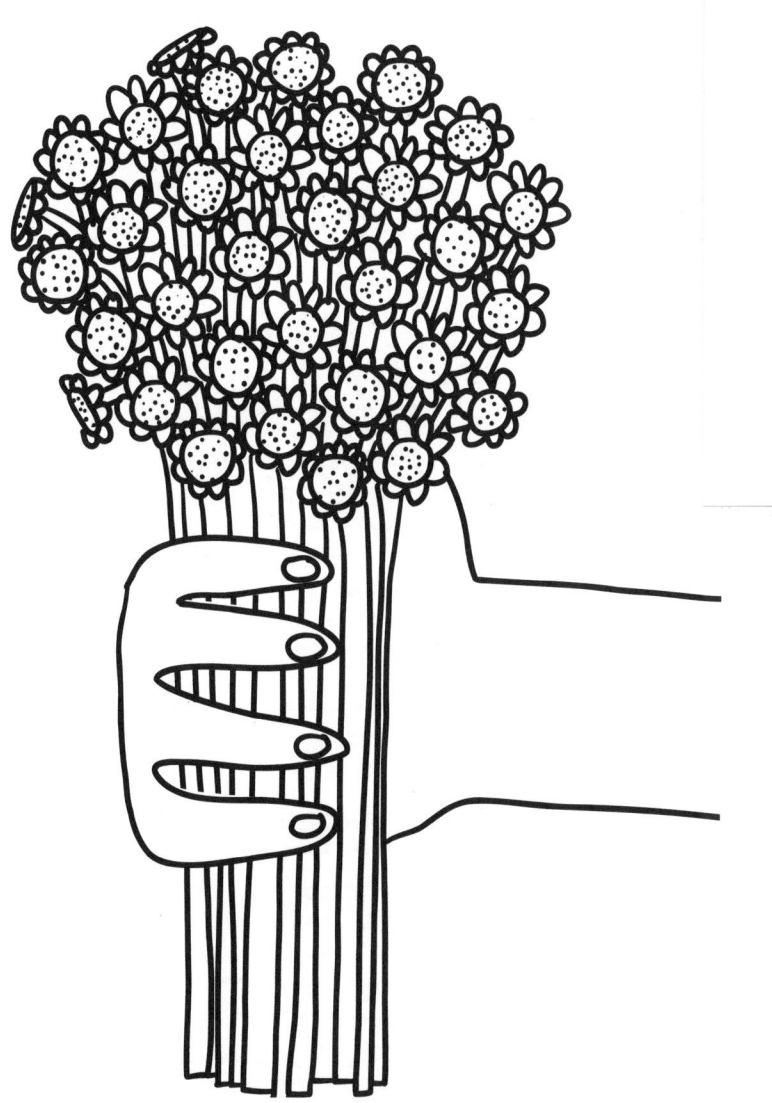

fold here so you can return →

NOTES

BEFORE I FELT:

AFTER I FEEL:

NEXT TIME I'D CHANGE:

ROOM SCAN

Sit down.
Take a deep breath.

Look at the room or space you are in.

Move your eyes from one surface to the next and one object to the next.

Mentally inventory and say the names of everything you see in your head (chair, cup, plant).

Go slowly, and stay focused on the immediate, tangible things around you.

fold here so you can return →

NOTES

BEFORE I FELT:

AFTER I FEEL:

NEXT TIME I'D CHANGE:

TAPPING TO RELEASE ANXIETY

Identify what you're feeling (e.g., I am anxious, overwhelmed, etc.).

Take a deep breath.

Begin tapping in a series of short, quick, repetitive taps, using this guide:

1. Use 4 fingers on your dominant hand to tap:

2. Use your index and middle fingers on both hands to tap:

3. Use your index and middle fingers on your dominant hand to tap:

fold here so you can return →

TAPPING
(part 2)

4. Use your index and middle fingers on both hands to tap:

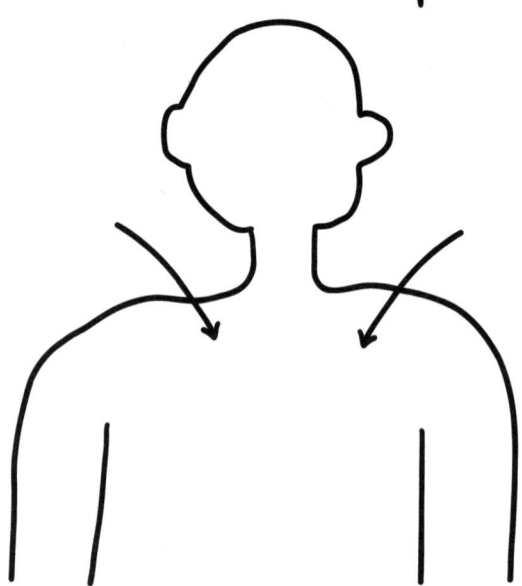

5. Use 4 fingers on your dominant hand to tap:

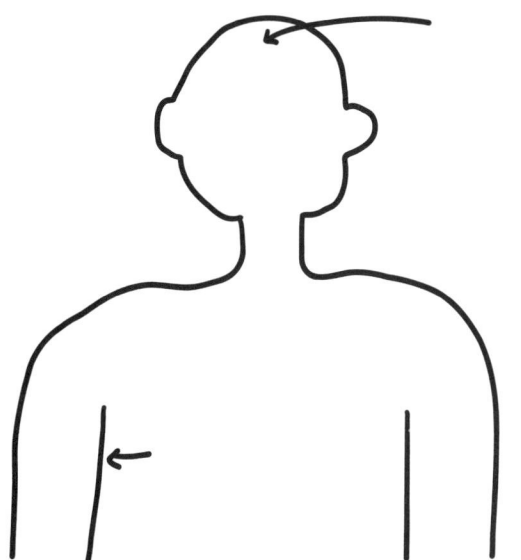

Tap each meridian point for the duration of this mantra:

"I am feeling_____."
"It's okay to feel_____."
"I accept myself fully."

fold here so you can return →

NOTES

BEFORE I FELT:

AFTER I FEEL:

NEXT TIME I'D CHANGE:

A BRISK WALK

Set a timer for 10 minutes.

"tick, tick"

Go outside. Take a deep breath and observe how your body feels. Notice any tense spots.

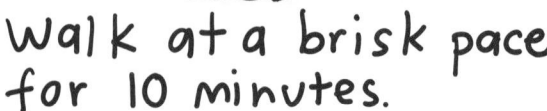

Walk at a brisk pace for 10 minutes.

Breathe naturally.

When the 10 minutes are up, take another deep breath and observe how your body feels.

NOTES

BEFORE I FELT:

AFTER I FEEL:

NEXT TIME I'D CHANGE:

BREATHING IN SCENT

Choose a favorite essential oil. Orange, peppermint, lavender, and tea tree are all good options.

tea tree

lavender

Run a hot shower. Get in.

peppermint   orange

Let the steam fill the shower. Place a few drops of the essential oil directly onto the shower floor.

As the aroma fills the shower and mixes with the steam, take several deep breaths in through your nose, exhaling each time through your mouth.

Let the scent transport you to another time and place.

fold here so you can return →

NOTES

BEFORE I FELT:

AFTER I FEEL:

NEXT TIME I'D CHANGE:

NERVOUS SYSTEM RESET

(From polyvagal theory to calm the vagus nerve)

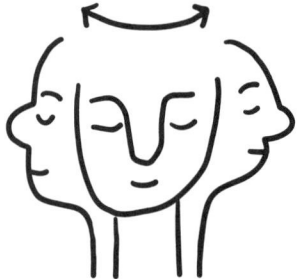

Sit down. Turn your head from side to side. Notice any tense spots.

Now lie down on your back, interlacing your fingers and cradling the back of your head.

Without moving your head,
look to the right for 30
seconds, then to the left
for 30 seconds.

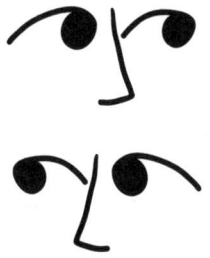

Repeat, moving your eyes
from side to side 30 seconds
at a time until you sigh,
swallow, or yawn.
Sit up. Turn your head from
side to side. Notice if
anything has shifted.

fold here so you can return →

NOTES

BEFORE I FELT:

AFTER I FEEL:

NEXT TIME I'D CHANGE:

SAVASANA

Lie on your back.
You can cushion your
body with a yoga mat
or blanket if you like.

Set a timer for 10 minutes
Let your feet splay open.
Rest your arms at your
sides with your palms
facing upward.

Close your eyes. Focus on
the way the ground feels
beneath you.

As your mind strays to
your to-do list or what's
stressing you, try to refocus
on the way the ground
feels.

When the timer goes off,
slowly blink open your
eyes. Wiggle your toes.

Take a big stretch from
head to toe.

Lie there as long as you
need to/can before
getting up.

fold here so you can return →

NOTES

BEFORE I FELT:

AFTER I FEEL:

NEXT TIME I'D CHANGE:

5-4-3-2-1
BACK INTO YOUR BODY

Take a deep breath.
Look around and notice:

5 things you can see
(rain, sofa, plants)

4 things you can feel
(clothes, chair, wind)

3 things you can hear
(cars, birds, breath)

2 things you can smell
(your body, lunch, flowers)

1 thing you can taste
(air, gum, tea)

fold here so you can return →

NOTES

BEFORE I FELT:

AFTER I FEEL:

NEXT TIME I'D CHANGE:

QUICK <u>CLOSE</u>

Ask a friend or partner if now is a good time.

If so, stare into each other's eyes for 4 minutes.

Lean in. Close your eyes and embrace for at least 30 seconds.

Feel the energy and heat of the other's body.

Notice how being held makes you feel.

fold here so you can return →

NOTES

BEFORE I FELT:

AFTER I FEEL:

NEXT TIME I'D CHANGE:

VISUALIZE STRESS FLOWING AWAY

Lie down in a comfortable spot.

Breathe naturally. Now, take a deep inhale.

As you exhale, imagine that your breath is carrying the stress away in waves.

With every inhale the wave crests. With every exhale, it breaks and flows away from you.

Picture the color of the waves and their temperature. The more detail you envision, the more effective this technique will be.

fold here so you can return →

NOTES

BEFORE I FELT:

AFTER I FEEL:

NEXT TIME I'D CHANGE:

WE ARE SO
LUCKY TO SPEND
OUR ONE AND ONLY
PRECIOUS LIFE
TOGETHER.

A BODY OF WATER

Find a body of water to sit near for at least 60 minutes.

This could be a lake, river, or even fountain.

Write down how you feel when you arrive.

Then, spend 20 minutes gazing upon it.

Spend 20 minutes writing about it.

(turn the page)

Spend 20 minutes
napping near it.

Write down how you
feel after 60 minutes.

Has anything changed
for you?

_____

_____

fold here so you can return →

Write for 20 minutes.

A MEMORY OF HAPPINESS

Sit in a comfortable position. Close your eyes.

Take 1 full inhale through your nose. Exhale through your mouth with a "haaaaa" sound.

Imagine a time when you felt truly happy. How did it feel in your body? Who were you with? What time of day was it? What was the weather like? Set the scene in as much detail as possible.

Linger in that memory for as long as you want.

Open your eyes and
write down how it felt.

fold here so you can return →

NOTES

BEFORE I FELT:

AFTER I FEEL:

NEXT TIME I'D CHANGE:

1 IDEAL DAY

Close your eyes and take 1 deep breath. Picture your ideal day.

Start in the morning. Imagine who's next to you, what your bed feels like, what kind of sheets are touching your skin, and what you eat for breakfast— then continue through the afternoon and evening, until you return back to bed.

Go through each step in your mind in as much detail as possible.

Now map out the day that you saw in this book and put it on the calendar to do in real life:

NOTES

BEFORE I FELT:

AFTER I FEEL:

NEXT TIME I'D CHANGE:

A FOREST BATH

Go for a walk in a
forest or a park for
at least 60 minutes.
Look for a place that
is thick with trees.

Walk until you find a
tree that you want to
spend some time with.

Lean on the tree, touch
its bark, and admire
its leaves and roots.

Breathe as you observe
the tree. Imagine that
with every inhale, you
are taking the tree's
exhale into your lungs.

fold here so you can return →

NOTES

BEFORE I FELT:

AFTER I FEEL:

NEXT TIME I'D CHANGE:

DRAWING NUMBERS IN THE DARK

Set a timer for 60 minutes or skip the timer if you're doing this before bed.

Close your eyes. Take a deep breath.

With each inhale and exhale, draw a number in your mind's eye.
Go from 1 to 10.
Imagine that the numbers are made of glittering brushstrokes.

When you get to 10, repeat the process going backward.

Continue counting until you drift asleep or the timer goes off.

fold here so you can return →

NOTES

BEFORE I FELT:

AFTER I FEEL:

NEXT TIME I'D CHANGE:

BREATHE YOURSELF
TO SLEEP

Get ready for bed. Make it as nice of a ritual as possible, doing the things you like.

Lie down and get under the covers.

Slowly, scan your body from head to toe, mentally noticing each part: head, eyes, ears, nose, mouth, neck, shoulders, chest...

Take a deep breath in. Breathe out slowly through your nose and listen to the sound your breath makes. Focus on the softness of the sound and the way it rises and falls in your body.

fold here so you can return →

NOTES

BEFORE I FELT:

AFTER I FEEL:

NEXT TIME I'D CHANGE:

YOUR BREATH IS YOUR GUIDE

Now that you've breathed through it, take a moment to imagine your breath as emotions that are filled with color. What does angry breath look like? What about smooth, even breath? Paint the colors you associate with your breath when you are experiencing these emotions:

Sad

Delighted

Anxious

Calm

Happy

Relieved

Do they also have a shape? Draw that, too.

Use this visual guide to aid your breathing as you return to these exercises over time.

GRATITUDE LIST

From us: To Lauren Appleton, our editor: Working with you is like a breath of fresh air. We are so grateful for your encouragement, your steadiness, and your insight. Thanks for giving us a second book.

To Nicole Tourtelot, our agent: Thank you for sparking so many of the ideas in this book, including the Boat Send-Off. It feels important to note that Nicole also suggested watching videos of hamsters as a method to relax, and although we couldn't fit that into the book, we highly recommend it.

From Vera: I would like to thank my mom for teaching me the Body Scan when I was a little girl and couldn't fall asleep. Making your body feel like jelly is her stroke of brilliance. I love you, Mom.

To Carissa: You're the voice in my head that believes in me when I'm unable to do it for myself. I wish we were still neighbors, eating cake together in the sun.

To Rob and Luca: You are the breath that fills my lungs. It is impossible to separate my existence from yours, and I wouldn't want to. I love you so much.

From Carissa: I fill my hours trying to derive meaning from the randomness of life. It was luck that I met and fell in love with Vera. She is a rock that I believe in. A person who makes me feel deeply cared about and worth it. I am so grateful to know her. In 2021, when she moved from a few blocks away from our house in Oakland, California, to live her dreams in

Italy, I was both equally heartbroken and overjoyed for her. Vera, you make everything better.

And for M. I am trying to learn how to self-regulate for you. And for me. For us. Before you, I thought that love, the concept of love, was inherently conditional. That people who said they loved without boundaries or benchmarks were delusional. But I am unconditionally in love with you. The kind of love I wish I could show myself. And Josh, you're neat.

Lastly, to Robin Wright for funding *How to Breathe Underwater* (the first iteration of this book). For thinking it needed to be in the world.

FURTHER READING

We are absolutely thrilled that you decided to pick up this book, and we hope that you will use it for years to come. The world is full of stressors, but it is also full of helpers. Here are a few of our favorites:

The 5 Resets: Rewire Your Brain and Body for Less Stress and More Resilience, by Aditi Nerurkar, MD

All About Love: New Visions, by bell hooks

The Body Keeps the Score: Brain, Mind, and Body in the Healing of Trauma, by Bessel van der Kolk, MD

Breath: The New Science of a Lost Art, by James Nestor

Draw Your Feelings: A Creative Journal to Help Connect with Your Emotions through Art, by Rukmini Poddar

Feel Something, Make Something: A Guide to Collaborating with Your Emotions, by Caitlin Metz

How We Heal: Uncover Your Power and Set Yourself Free, by Alexandra Elle

Permission to Rest: Revolutionary Practices for Healing, Empowerment, and Collective Care, by Ashley Neese

The Polyvagal Theory: Neurophysiological Foundations of Emotions, Attachment, Communication, and Self-Regulation, by Steven W. Porges

Practices for Embodied Living: Experiencing the Wisdom of Your Body, by Hillary L. McBride, PhD

Pure Colour: A Novel, by Sheila Heti

The Sunny Nihilist: A Declaration of the Pleasure of Pointlessness, by Wendy Syfret

What It Takes to Heal: How Transforming Ourselves Can Change the World, by Prentis Hemphill

Wintering: The Power of Rest and Retreat in Difficult Times, by Katherine May

ABOUT US

Carissa Potter is an artist and the founder of People I've Loved, a social media presence and stationery line that bridges the gaps between people by helping them have authentic and sometimes difficult conversations. In 2021, Carissa was named one of the 50 People and Companies Inspiring the Working Not Working Community Right Now and one of *Cosmopolitan*'s 24 People (Genuinely) Making the World a Better Place. She lives with her partner, father, mother-in-law, and daughter in Oakland, California. This is her fourth book.

    Vera Kachouh is a writer based in Italy. Her essays have been published in *Memoir Land* and *Electric Literature*. This is her second book.

AND THEN
FOR NO
APPARENT
REASON,
I BEGAN
TO FEEL
BETTER.

SOMEDAY, WE'LL LOOK BACK ON THIS TIME AND WONDER HOW WE GOT THROUGH IT. WE HAVE NO IDEA HOW WE'LL DO IT.

WE HAD TO, SO WE DID.

NOTES

NOTES

NOTES

NOTES

ATHE IN BREATHE OUT BR
IN BREATHE OUT BREATH
ATHE IN BREATHE OUT BRE
IN BREATHE OUT BREATHE
REATHE IN BREATHE OUT B
E IN BREATHE OUT BREATH
ATHE IN BREATHE OUT BRE
IN BREATHE OUT BREATHE
ATHE IN BREATHE OUT BR
IN BREATHE OUT BREATH
ATHE IN BREATHE OUT BRE
IN BREATHE OUT BREATHE
REATHE IN BREATHE OUT B
E IN BREATHE OUT BREATH
ATHE IN BREATHE OUT BRE
IN BREATHE OUT BREATHE
EATHE IN BREATHE OUT BR
E IN BREATHE OUT BREATH
ATHE IN BREATHE OUT BRE
IN BREATHE OUT BREATHE
EATHE IN BREATHE OUT B